Christina & Chand –
A Beautiful
Friendship

As Different as the Sun & the Moon

Mona Sabah

A "Go & Make Disciples of All Nations!" Series Book

GETHSEMANE
PRESS

DEDICATION

This book is dedicated to my lovely children and grandchildren. May you walk with the Lord humbly and shine the light of Christ all the days of your life.

I also dedicate this to my church family. Thank you for the love you have for Christ and for one another. May the Lord help us to proclaim that we are saved by grace alone, through faith alone, in Christ alone, as revealed by Scripture alone, to the glory of God alone.

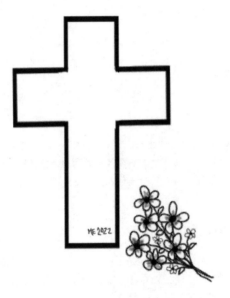

TO THE READER:

1 Peter 3:15 (ESV) says, "But in your hearts revere Christ as Lord. Always be prepared to give an answer to everyone who asks you to give the reason for the hope that you have. But do this with gentleness and respect." This is a verse that should motivate all Christians to prepare to give answers in defense of their faith. Evangelism means to Share the Good News of the Gospel. Many times, Evangelism and Defending the Faith (Apologetics) go hand in hand.

This book is to help you talk to people from other cultures and to share the Gospel. It is meant for all ages from 1 to 100 years old. I have provided a list of Islamic Terms and a pronunciation key at the back of the book. Also, there's an easy to way to explain the Gospel towards the end of the book. I hope these tools and the conversation between the characters in this book will equip you and the child in your life to make disciples for Jesus Christ.

In this book, Christina makes a new friend at school named Chand. Christina's mother helps to bridge the gap between their beliefs and gives Christina an understanding of her friend's culture, traditions, and differences between Islam and Christianity.

In this series, Christina represents a Christian who meets others who are different from her. Join her as she learns about their culture and religion. See how understanding the culture can help reach new people in her life who do not know the beauty of the Gospel.

 When you see the Crescent Moon (a symbol of Islam), it might be a way to connect with your Muslim friend!

☀ **Christina: Mommy! I met a new girl at school today!**

💜 **Mom: That's wonderful, Christina!**

Christina: Her name is Chand *[ch aah nd]* and it means Moon in her language. She is pretty like the Moon. I'm so glad we can be friends!

I asked her why she wears a scarf on her head. She said it's a HIJAB and she wears it because she is a Muslim.

Mommy, What does "Muslim" mean?

💜 **Mom: A MUSLIM is a person whose religion is ISLAM.**

☀ **Christina: What does ISLAM mean?**

♥ **Mom: It means "To Submit" (to the will of ALLAH – name of Muslim God in Arabic).**

Christina: Chand said that Christians and Muslims are the same. So, will she be at our church this Sunday?

 Mom: You can always invite her to come to church with us, Christina. But Christians and Muslims are very different.

Your new friend will most likely go to a MOSQUE or a MASJID to pray on Friday. A Mosque is a gathering place for prayer.

Maybe you could ask her what she does at a Mosque on Friday and how she prays to Allah? That way she can help you understand.

Christina: Oh, do Muslims Pray also?

 Mom: Yes, they do! They have 5 set times a day when they pray in Arabic to Allah. This is a part of the good works they are required to do.

💜 **But as Christians, we pray in the morning, at lunch, at school, in the car, with our friends and at bedtime [1 Thessalonians 5:17]. We can pray at any time, any place and in any language to our Lord.**

☀ **Christina: Chand said her holy book is called the QURAN and it's written in Arabic. Can I bring my BIBLE to show her how we study God's commands?**

♥ **Mom: Of course! That is a great way to share about Jesus!**

☾ **Maybe we could give Chand her own copy of the Bible for her Birthday or Christmas gift?**

Christina: Well, Chand said she already knows about Jesus.

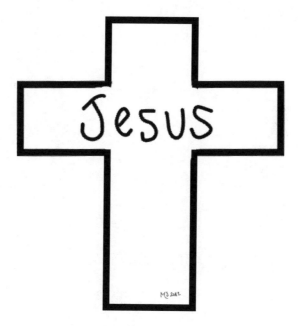

 Mom: Jesus ("ISA" in Arabic) in the Quran is not the same Jesus we worship in the Bible. Muslims believe that Jesus was only a prophet.

☀ Christina: But... *Jesus is God!*

♥ Mom: Yes, Christians believe that Jesus is God because He said He is [John 1:1 & John 8:58]!

Christina: If Muslims don't believe the same things as we do, will they go to Heaven, Mommy?

 Mom: Muslims believe their good works will get them to Heaven. But the Bible tells us that only through the work Jesus did on the cross on our behalf can make us right with God [Matthew 1:21, Acts 4:12, 1 Tim 2:5].

Islam says that every Muslim is required to do all 5 of these Pillars of Islam perfectly so they can go to Heaven. These are the "good works" they believe in.

The Pillars are:
1. Belief in 1 God, Allah
2. Praying 5X a day
3. Fasting for Ramadan
4. Giving Charity
5. Pilgrimage to Mecca (HAJJ)

Christina: Mommy, Chand didn't eat or drink anything at lunch today. I tried to give her my sandwich but she said, "no thank you." Why didn't she eat?

 Mom: She may be fasting for RAMADAN. It's one of the 5 Pillars.

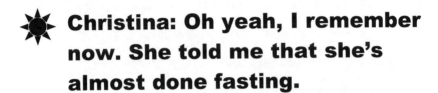 **Christina: Oh yeah, I remember now. She told me that she's almost done fasting.**

Then she said her family will have a big party to celebrate the end of Ramadan, called Eid!

Mom: That sounds like fun! Chand and her family will be celebrating 2 Eid Festivals this year. There is Eid al Fitr (after 30 days of Ramadan) and Eid al Adha (after the Hajj Pilgrimage to Mecca, which is one of the 5 Pillars).

Christina: Oh! Is Eid like Christmas?

 Mom: While both celebrations have presents, they focus on very different things.

Maybe you can ask Chand why they celebrate Eid & share why we celebrate Christmas?

Then you could share that we celebrate Christmas to honor the birth of our Savior Jesus Christ.

He came into the world He created. He was born of a virgin [Luke 2:11].
He existed before time because He is the Eternal Creator [John 1:10].
But the story doesn't end there!

The purpose of Jesus' life is shown on **RESURRECTION SUNDAY (Easter)**. We celebrate this because Jesus died on the cross but after 3 days, He was victoriously raised from the tomb [Luke 24:6-7 & 1 Cor 15:4].

JESUS is ALIVE TODAY!

This means those who belong to Him have eternal life [John 3:16]. God forgives us for all the bad things we have done only if we trust and have faith in Jesus [John 5:24 & 14:6].

Christina: Mommy, do you think Chand knows that Jesus died on the cross but is alive today?

Mom: Probably not, but this is a great thing to share with her tomorrow at school!

Christina, Let's pray together for Chand and all Muslims, that we can love them best by sharing the Good News of Jesus and that she doesn't have to do any of the work to make God happy with her because Jesus died on the cross. He did everything perfectly and we are able to go to Heaven through Him. For those who trust Jesus will live forever in Heaven with Him.

ME 2022

PRAYER: Dear Lord, help us to love people as Christ loves His children. Help us to share about who He truly is with those who don't know Him. Please give us the chance to speak to others with gentleness and respect. We ask that You open their hearts so they will understand. In Jesus' name we pray. Amen.

GOSPEL ARROWS
An Easy Way to Remember the Gospel

 Man cannot work his way to God, so God came down and dwelt with us (Immanuel = Jesus)

 Jesus Christ died on the cross to pay for our sins

 He was buried in a tomb

 After 3 days, He rose again from the dead & went up to Heaven

 We need to confess our sins, repent (turn back), & trust in Jesus Christ to save us from the punishment for breaking God's laws

Jesus is coming back to judge the world & take His people to Heaven to live with Him

ISLAMIC WORDS

ADAH [ud-hah]	Sacrifice (Eid al Adha)
ALLAH [ul laah]	Name of Muslim God in Arabic
EID [eed]	Festival or Celebration
FASTING	To not eat or drink from sunrise to sunset during Ramadan for Muslims
FIVE PILLARS	A list of religious duties (works) Muslims do to get to Heaven – Allah only, Prayer 5X, Fasting, Alms (Charity) & Hajj
HAJJ [huj]	Pilgrimage to Mecca. One of the 5 Pillars
HIJAB [hee job]	A barrier or partition. A head covering for Muslim women
ISA [ee saw]	Arabic name for Jesus in the Quran
ISLAM [ees lahm]	Religion that worships Allah
MASJID [moss jed]	Another word for Mosque
MOSQUE [mosskh]	A place of worship and prayer for Muslims
MUSLIM [moose slim]	One who submits to the will of Allah
PROPHET	One who brings God's message
QURAN [koo ron]	Islam's Holy Book (also "Koran") that contains right or wrong behavior for Muslims
RAMADAN [rah ma don]	30 Days of Fasting (from sunrise to sunset). One of the 5 Pillars

Please look for other books with Christina & friends in the "GO & MAKE DISCIPLES OF ALL NATIONS!" Series Books

BIBLE VERSES

(as used in book)

1 Thessalonians 5:17 – Pray without ceasing

Matthew 1:21 - She will bear a son, and you shall call his name Jesus, for he will save his people from their sins.

Acts 4:12 - And there is salvation in no one else, for there is no other name under heaven given among men by which we must be saved.

1 Timothy 2:5 - For there is one God, and there is one mediator between God and men, the man Christ Jesus

Luke 2:11 - For unto you is born this day in the city of David a Savior, who is Christ the Lord.

John 1:10 - He was in the world, and the world was made through him, yet the world did not know him.

Luke 24:6-7 - He is not here, but has risen. Remember how he told you, while he was still in Galilee, that the Son of Man must be delivered into the hands of sinful men and be crucified and on the third day rise."

1 Cor 15:4 - that he was buried, that he was raised on the third day in accordance with the Scriptures,

John 3:16 - For God so loved the world, that he gave his only Son, that whoever believes in him should not perish but have eternal life.

John 5:24 - Truly, truly, I say to you, whoever hears my word and believes him who sent me has eternal life. He does not come into judgment, but has passed from death to life.

John 14:6 - Jesus said to him, "I am the way, and the truth, and the life. No one comes to the Father except through me.

ABOUT THE AUTHOR

Mona Sabah was born in the Middle East, lived in 5 countries & speaks 3 languages. She was a Muslim for 35 years and is now an ambassador for Christ. . Mona lived in the United States for 25 years without an authentic witness to the pure Gospel.

She moved to the United States from Pakistan, lived in a Muslim community in California and then thwarted the tradition of arranged marriage by marrying an American. After the events of 9/11, she decided to delve deeper into her faith by reading the Quran and praying to Allah.

When she encountered the chapter on Jesus (Isa-Surah Maryam), she couldn't figure out why this prophet was so different. She prayed to God to give her the truth and show her the way. He pointed to One: Jesus Christ.

She writes and speaks about her salvation and stresses the importance of sharing the Good News of Christ

She loves to draw, paint and sketch. She was thrilled to write a children's book that would use her scribblings for the glory of God!

She prays about opportunities to share her testimony about Jesus and teach others how to share the Gospel. If you would like her to speak at your event, please contact her through her Blog: monasabahbooks.com
Social Media: @monasabahbooks

OTHER BOOKS BY MONA SABAH:
From Isa to Christ
Reaching Muslims – A Christian's Guide to Islam
Half in Islam, Whole in Jesus – A Woman's Worth

PEOPLE I NEED TO PRAY FOR: